Rockschool Ba

Companion Guide

Acknowledgements

Published by Rockschool Ltd. © 2007

Catalogue Number: RSK100602

Compiled by: Jason Woolley www.jasonwoolleymusic.co.uk

Edited by: Simon Pitt & Peter Scott

Music engraving and layouts: Simon & Jennie Troup www.DigitalMusicArt.com

Audio production: Jason Woolley

Syllabus Manager: Jeremy Ward

Cover design: Gillian Harding www.fuelcreativity.com

Printed and bound in the United Kingdom by Caligraving Ltd, Thetford, Norfolk

CDs manufactured in the United Kingdom by Branded Media Ltd, Basingstoke, Hampshire

Exclusive Distributors: Music Sales Ltd www.musicroom.com

Visit the Rockschool website at www.rockschool.co.uk

Telephone: 020 8332 6303

Fax: 020 8332 6297

Welcome to the Bass Companion Guide

Welcome to the Rockschool *Companion Guide* for Bass. This *Companion Guide* is designed to give teachers, learners and candidates multiple examples of the unseen tests that are to be found within each Rockschool grade exam from Grades 1-8. The *Companion Guide* contains between three and six examples of each of the following tests:

- Sight Reading (Grades 1-5)

- Improvisation & Interpretation (Grades 1-5)*

- Ear Tests (Grades 1-8)*

- Quick Study Pieces (Grades 6-8)*

All of the test examples marked (*) can be found on the audio CDs accompanying this *Companion Guide*. The quick study pieces (QSPs) come in two audio versions: one with a full mix of the QSP and one with the bass part removed. Please refer to the track listings given in the text.

In addition, you will find examples of the kinds of general musicianship questions that candidates are asked in each grade exam from Grades 1-8.

Teachers, learners and candidates should also refer to the Rockschool *Syllabus Guide* for Bass where they will find the technical specifications for each section of the exam syllabus, including those parts (the performance pieces and the technical exercises) not covered by this *Companion Guide*. The Bass specifications can be found in the *Guitar, Bass and Drums Syllabus Guide* on pages 16-25. References to the relevant sections of the Bass *Syllabus Guide* can be found in each section below.

The purpose of the *Companion Guide* is to give candidates practice examples of the kinds of tests they will encounter in the exam. In the case of the sight reading, improvisation & interpretation and ear tests, we have created examples within each grade, which offer candidates a progressive level of difficulty within a single grade: the first test example will be relatively simple when compared with the actual tests used in the exam, while the last example will be relatively more difficult. We have done this with the aim of aiding candidate confidence when faced with the tests in the exam.

If you have any queries about the syllabus for Bass (or any other exam syllabus offered by Rockschool in electric guitar, drums, vocals, piano or our Music Practitioners qualifications) then please do not hesitate to call us on **020 8332 6303** or email us at: **info@rockschool.co.uk**. The Rockschool website, **www.rockschool.co.uk**, has detailed information on all aspects of our examinations, including examination regulations, detailed marking schemes and marking criteria as well as handy tips on how to get the most out of the performance pieces.

Sight Reading

Candidates attempting Grades 1-5 inclusive have a choice of taking either the sight reading or the improvisation & interpretation test in the exam. Six examples of the types of tests required in the exam are shown below. The full technical specifications of each test offered to candidates in the exam can be found in the Bass *Syllabus Guide* on page 21. Please note that in Grades 4 and 5 each sight reading test also contains two bars of improvisation & interpretation.

You will be asked to prepare a sight reading test which is given to you by the examiner. This test may be in one of the following styles: blues or rock (Grades 1-3) or blues, rock, funk or jazz (Grades 4 & 5). The examiner will allow you 90 seconds to prepare the test and will set the tempo on a metronome. You can choose to play with or without the metronome. TAB fingerings are given along with standard notation in all sight reading tests.

Grade 1

The following examples are indicative of the types of test you will be given in the Grade 1 exam.

Example 1

Example 2

Example 3

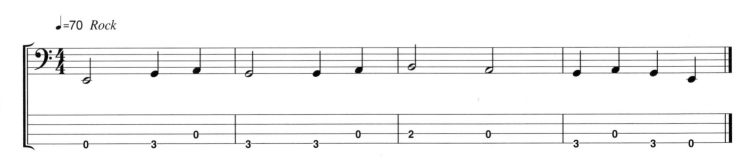

Example 4

Example 5

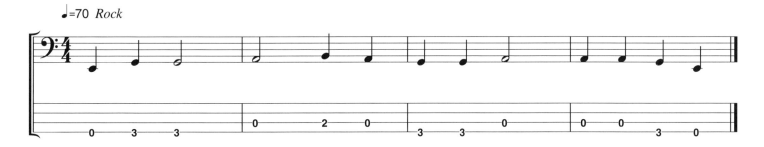

Example 6

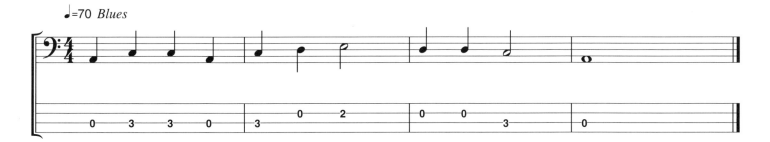

Grade 2

The following examples are indicative of the types of test you will be given in the Grade 2 exam.

Example 1

Example 2

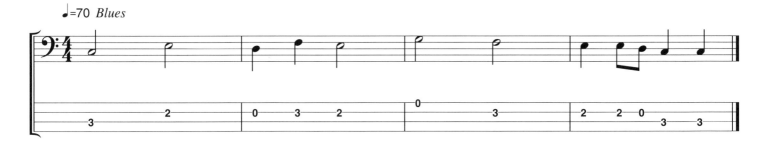

Example 3

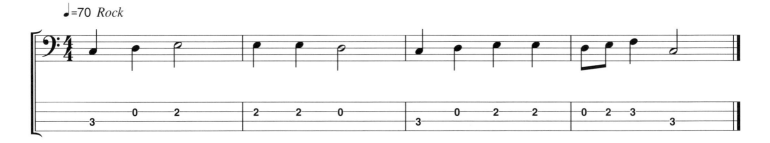

Example 4

Example 5

Example 6

Grade 3

The following examples are indicative of the types of test you will be given in the Grade 3 exam.

Example 1

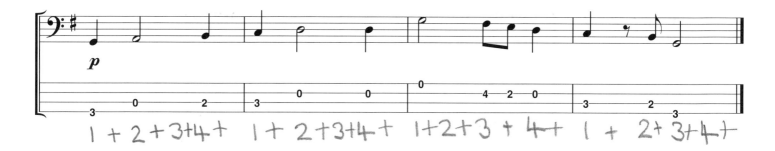

Example 2

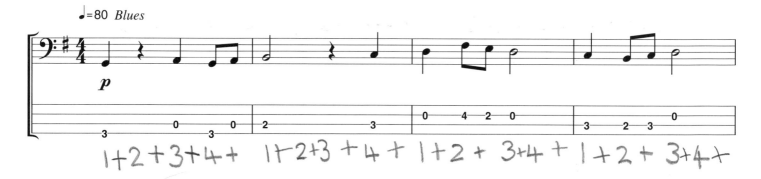

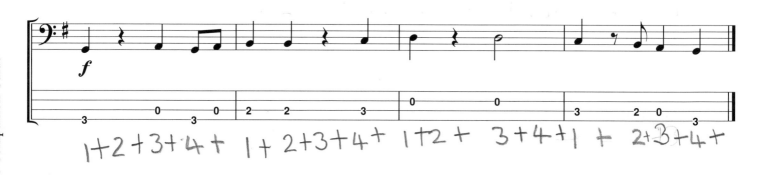

Example 3

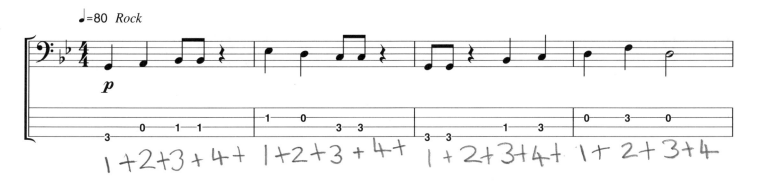

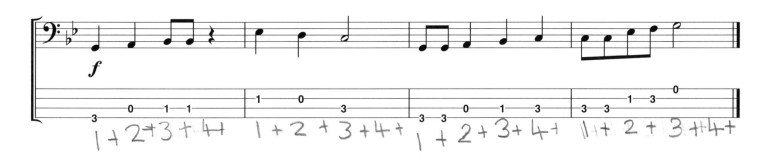

Example 4

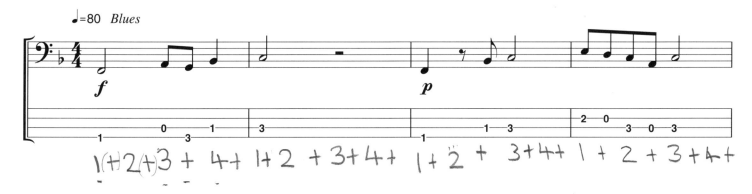

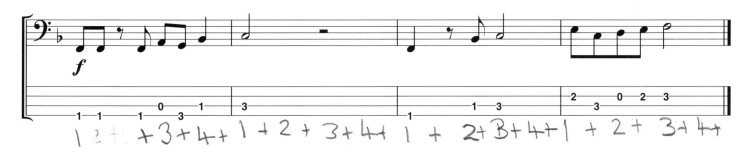

Example 5

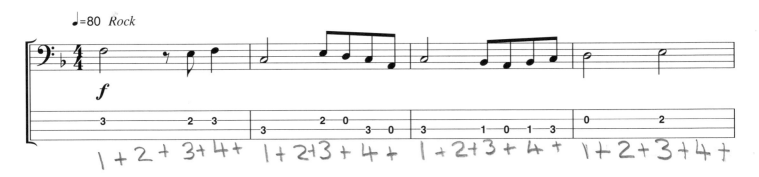

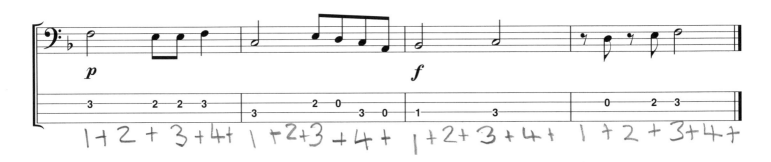

Example 6

Grade 4

The following examples are indicative of the types of test you will be given in the Grade 4 exam. Please note that in Grade 4, the sight reading tests contain a small amount of improvisation & interpretation. This consists of a two bar section to be found at the end of each test.

Example 1

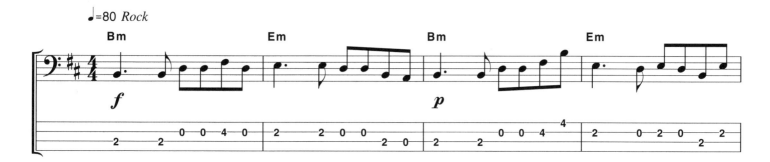

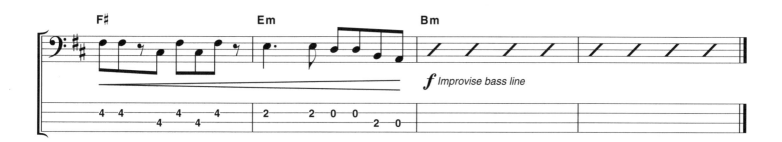

Example 2

Example 3

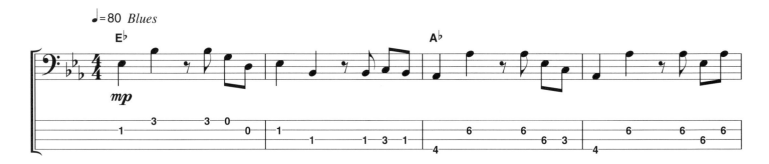

Example 4

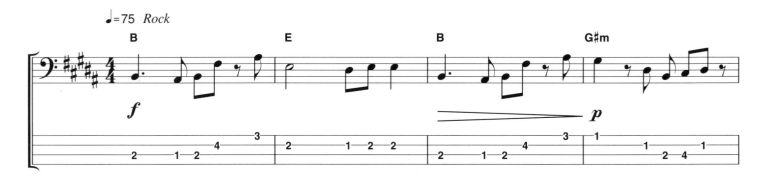

Example 5

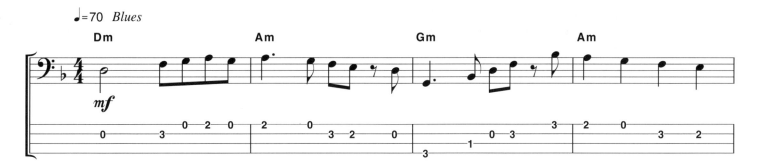

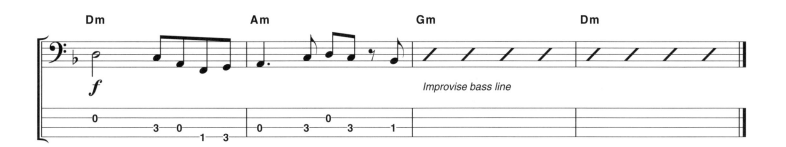

Example 6

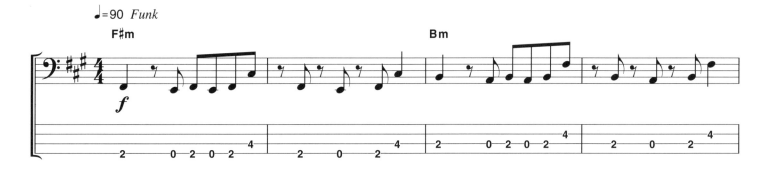

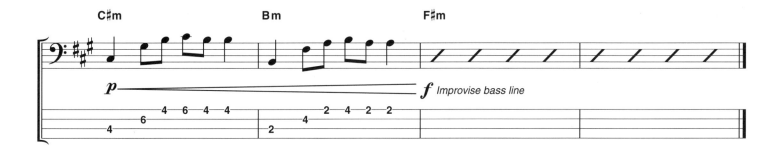

Grade 5

The following examples are indicative of the types of test you will be given in the Grade 5 exam. Please note that in Grade 5, the sight reading tests contain a small amount of improvisation & interpretation. This consists of a two bar section to be found at the end of each test.

Example 1

Example 2

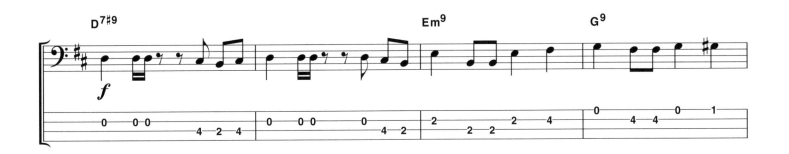

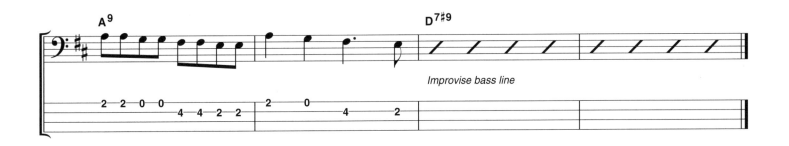

Example 3

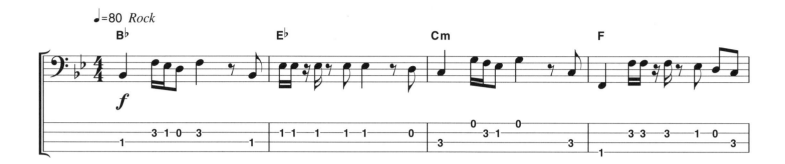

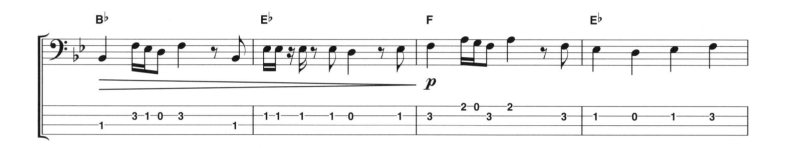

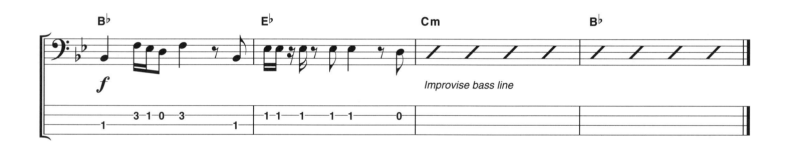

Example 4

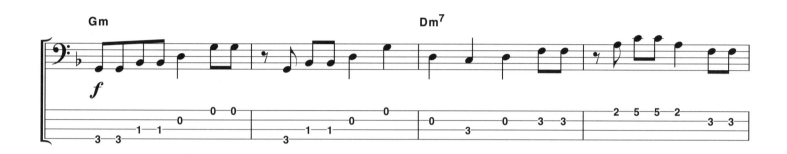

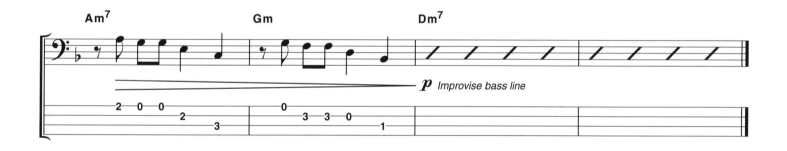

Example 5

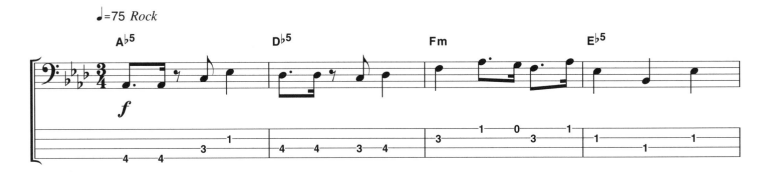

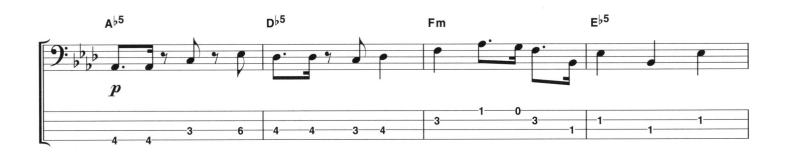

Example 6

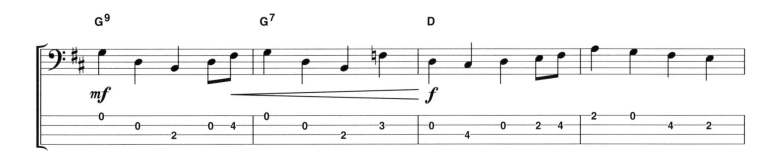

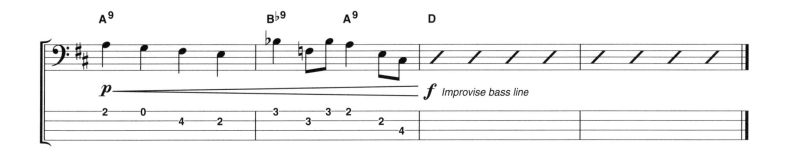

Improvisation & Interpretation

Candidates attempting Grades 1-5 inclusive have a choice of taking either the sight reading or the improvisation & interpretation test in the exam. Six examples of the types of tests required in the exam are shown below. The full technical specifications of each test can be found in the Bass *Syllabus Guide* on pages 21-22. Please note that in Grades 4 and 5 each improvisation & interpretation test also contains two bars of sight reading.

You will be asked to prepare an improvisation & interpretation test which is given to you by the examiner. This test may be in one of the following styles: blues or rock (Grades 1-3) or blues, rock, funk or jazz (Grades 4 & 5).

Grade 1

You will be asked to play an improvised line to a backing track of four bars. You have 30 seconds to prepare and then you will be allowed to practise through on the first playing of the backing track, before playing it to the examiner on the second playing of the backing track. This test is continuous with a one bar count in at the beginning and after the practice session.

Example 1
CD 1 Track 1

Example 2
CD 1 Track 2

Example 3
CD 1 Track 3

Example 4   CD 1 Track 4

Example 5   CD 1 Track 5

Example 6   CD 1 Track 6

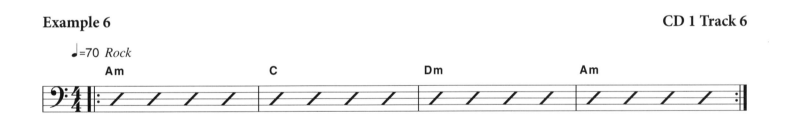

Grade 2

You will be asked to play an improvised line to a backing track of four bars. You have 30 seconds to prepare and then you will be allowed to practise through on the first playing of the backing track, before playing it to the examiner on the second playing of the backing track. This test is continuous with a one bar count in at the beginning and after the practice session.

Example 1   **CD 1 Track 7**

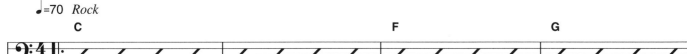

Example 2   **CD 1 Track 8**

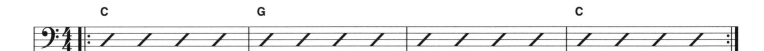

Example 3   **CD 1 Track 9**

Example 4

♩=70 *Rock*

Example 5

♩=70 *Funk Rock*

Example 6

♩=70 *Rock*

Grade 3

You will be asked to play an improvised line to a backing track of eight bars. You have 30 seconds to prepare and then you will be allowed to practise through on the first playing of the backing track, before playing it to the examiner on the second playing of the backing track. This test is continuous with a one bar count in at the beginning and after the practice session.

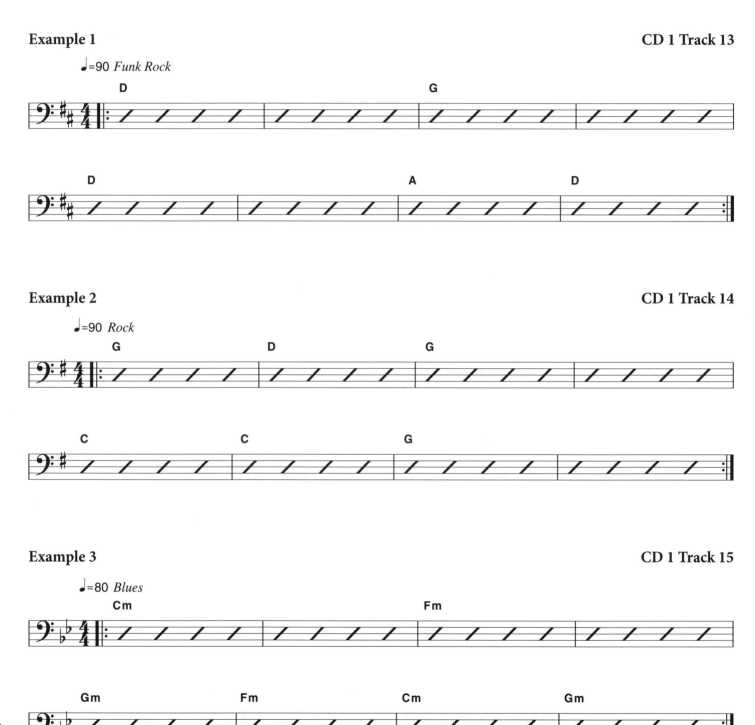

Example 1   **CD 1 Track 13**

Example 2   **CD 1 Track 14**

Example 3   **CD 1 Track 15**

Example 4

CD 1 Track 16

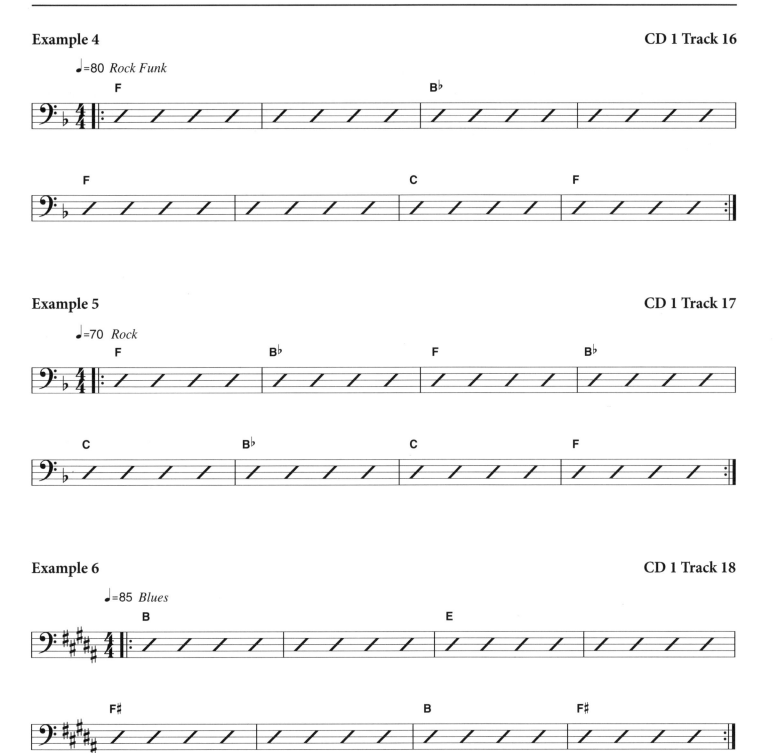

Example 5

CD 1 Track 17

Example 6

CD 1 Track 18

Grade 4

In Grade 4, the improvisation & interpretation tests contain a small amount of sight reading. This takes the form of a two bar bass line to be found at the beginning of each test. You will be asked to improvise a bassline using the chord sequence as indicated. This is played to a backing track of no more than eight bars. You have 30 seconds to prepare and then you will be allowed to practise through on the first playing of the backing track, before playing it to the examiner on the second playing of the backing track. This test is continuous with a one bar count in at the beginning and after the practice session.

Example 1   CD 1 Track 19

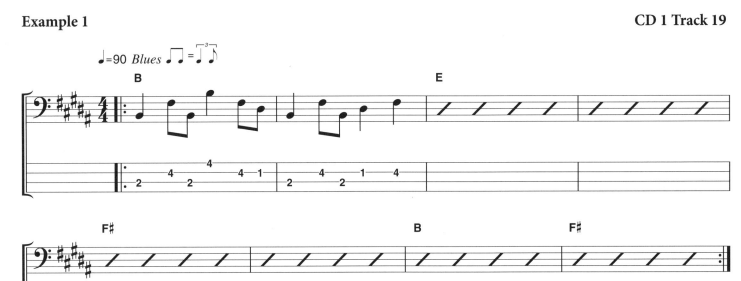

Example 2   CD 1 Track 20

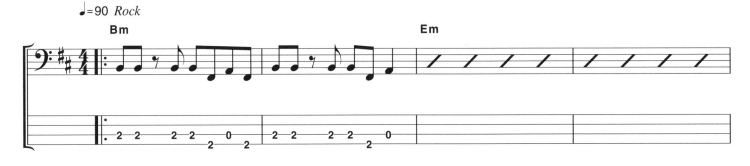

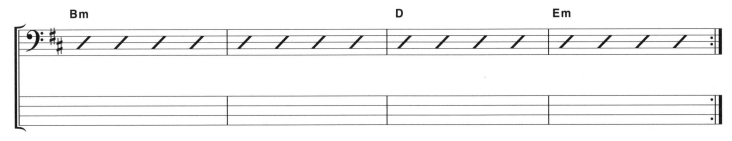

Example 3

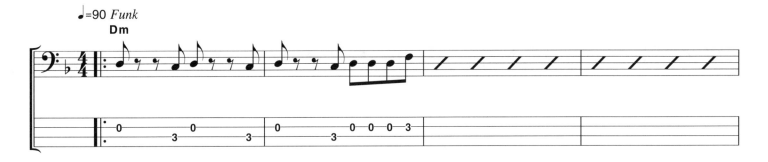

Example 4

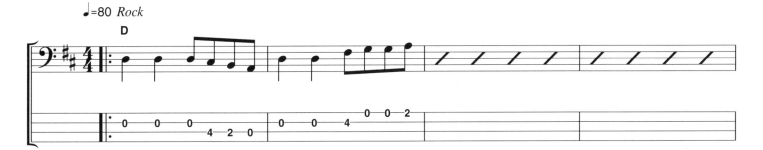

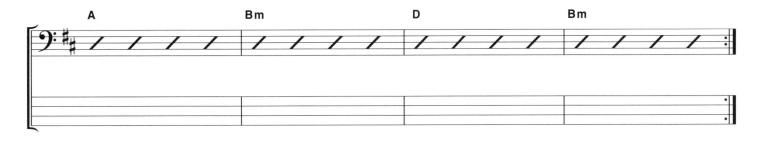

Example 5

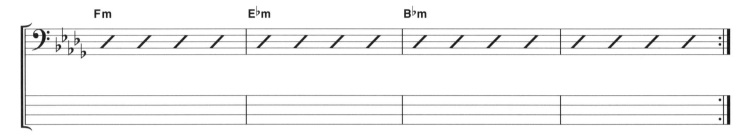

Example 6

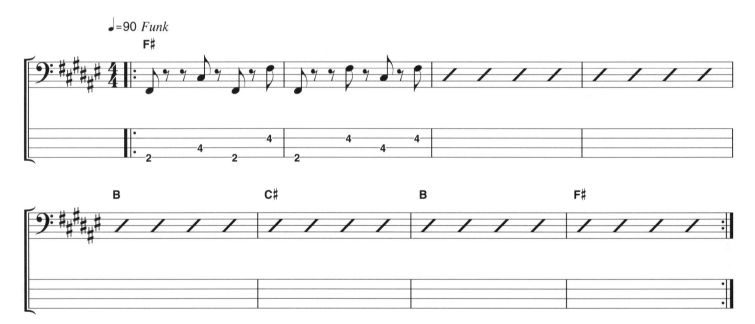

Grade 5

In Grade 5, the improvisation & interpretation tests contain a small amount of sight reading. This takes the form of a two bar bass line to be found at the beginning of each test. You will be asked to improvise a bassline using the chord sequence as indicated. This is played to a backing track of no more than twelve bars. You have 30 seconds to prepare and then you will be allowed to practise through on the first playing of the backing track, before playing it to the examiner on the second playing of the backing track. This test is continuous with a one bar count in at the beginning and after the practice session.

Example 1   CD 1 Track 25

Example 2   CD 1 Track 26

Example 3   CD 1 Track 27

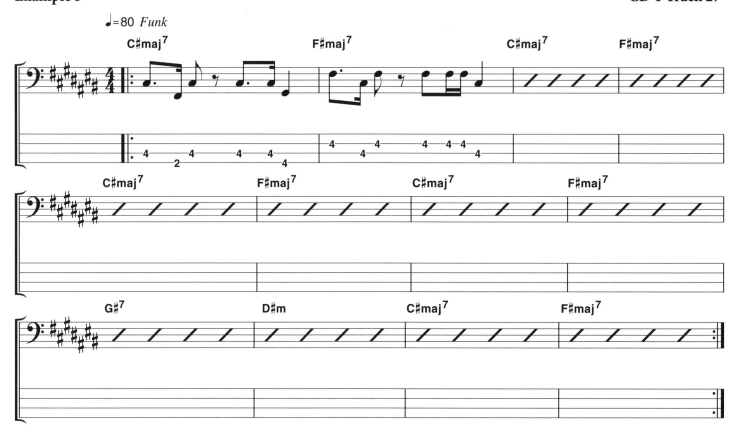

Example 4   CD 1 Track 28

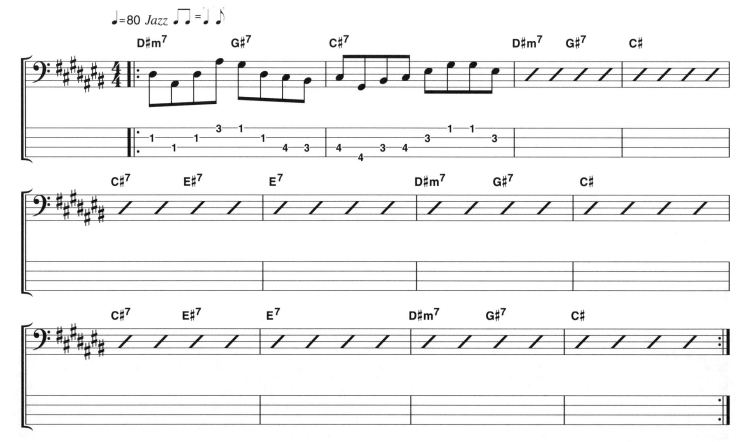

Example 5

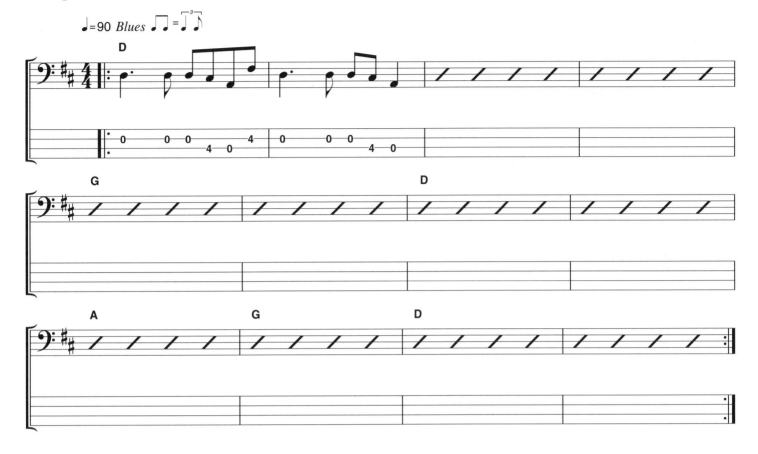

Example 6

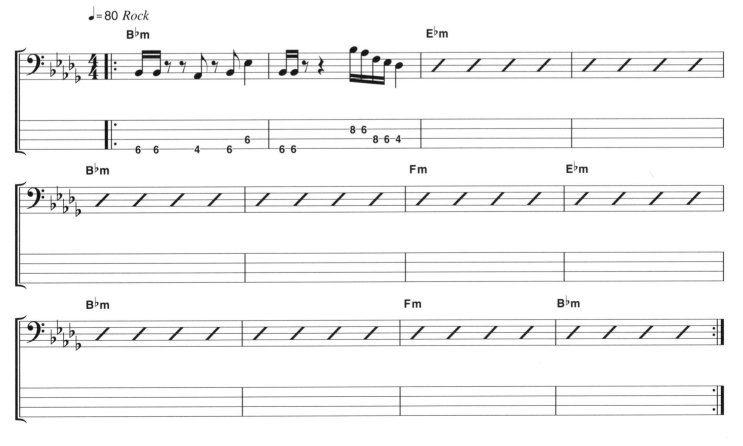

Ear Tests

You will be asked to play two ear tests in the exam. The tests are played on CD and use real instrument sounds. Each test is played to you by the examiner twice and you will play back Test 1 to either a drum backing (Grades 1-5) or to a guitar and drum backing (Grades 6-8). Test 2 is played back unaccompanied in Grades 1 and 2. You may use your instrument while the CD is playing. Technical specifications for the ear tests can be found in the Bass *Syllabus Guide* on pages 23-24.

Grade 1 Test 1: Melodic Recall

You will be asked to play back on your instrument a two bar melody composed from the first three notes of the E minor pentatonic scale (E, G & A). You will be given the tonic and told the starting note. The test will be played twice with a drum backing. There is a short break for you to practise and then the test will recommence. You will then play the melody in time to the drum backing. The test is continuous.

Example 1

CD 1 Track 31

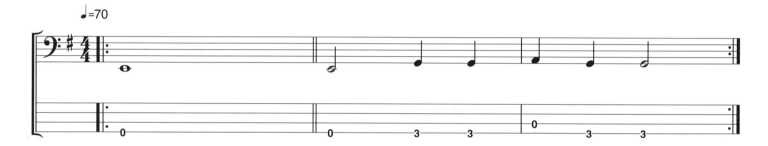

Example 2

CD 1 Track 32

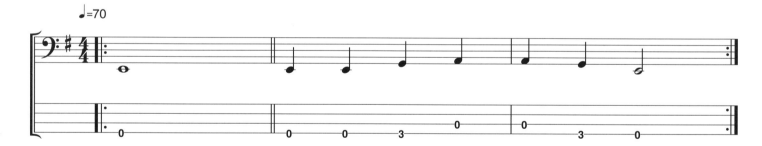

Example 3

CD 1 Track 33

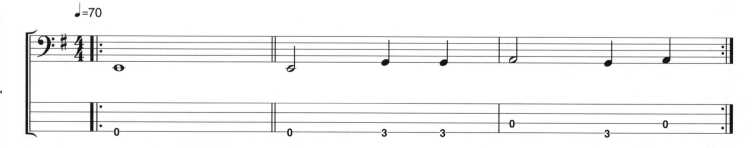

Example 4

Example 5

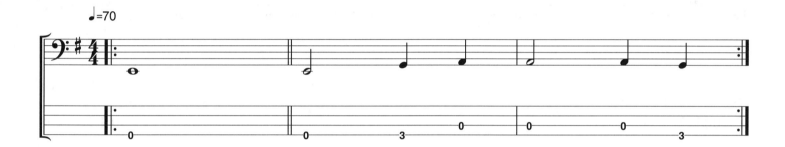

Example 6

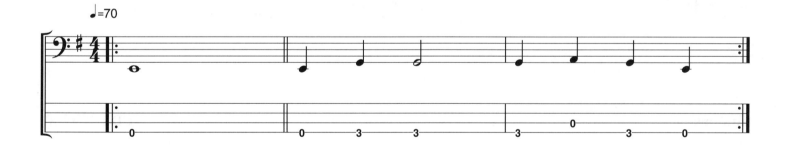

Grade 1 Test 2: Rhythmic Recall

You will be asked to play back on your instrument a two bar rhythm played on the bottom E string on the bass. The rhythm is played twice and then you will play it back unaccompanied to the examiner.

Example 1   **CD 1 Track 37**

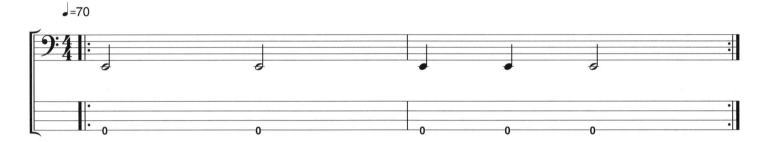

Example 2   **CD 1 Track 38**

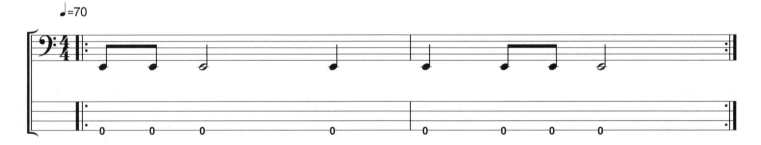

Example 3   **CD 1 Track 39**

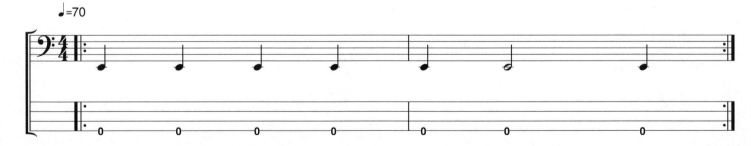

Example 4

Example 5

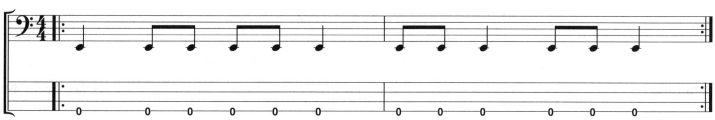

Example 6

Grade 2 Test 1: Melodic Recall

You will be asked to play back on your instrument a two bar melody composed from notes of the C major scale. You will be given the tonic and told the starting note. The test will be played twice with a drum backing. There is a short break for you to practise and then the test will recommence. You will then play the melody in time to the drum backing. The test is continuous.

Example 1   CD 1 Track 43

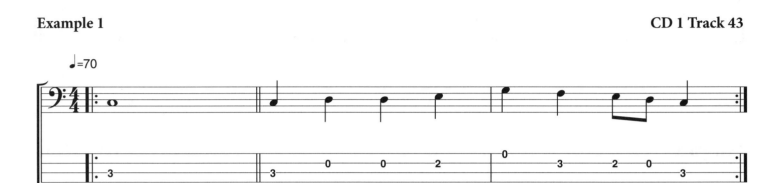

Example 2   CD 1 Track 44

Example 3   CD 1 Track 45

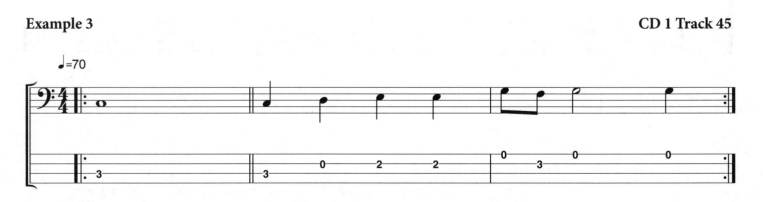

Example 4

CD 1 Track 46

Example 5

CD 1 Track 47

Example 6

CD 1 Track 48

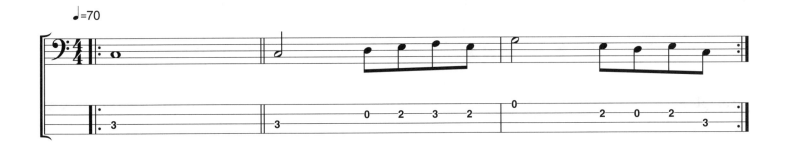

Grade 2 Test 2: Rhythmic Recall

You will be asked to play back on your instrument a two bar rhythm played on the E string on the bass. The rhythm is played twice and then you will play it back unaccompanied to the examiner.

Example 1   **CD 1 Track 49**

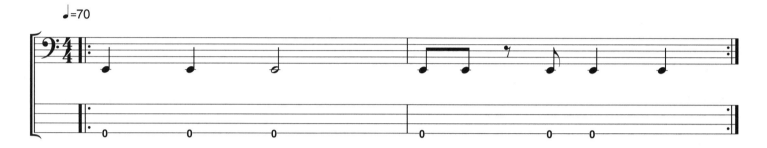

Example 2   **CD 1 Track 50**

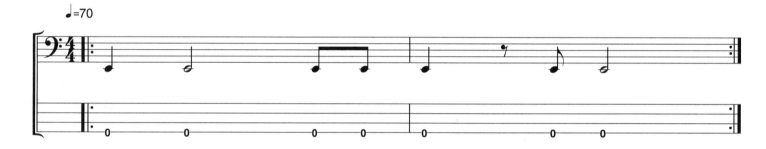

Example 3   **CD 1 Track 51**

Example 4

CD 1 Track 52

Example 5

CD 1 Track 53

Example 6

CD 1 Track 54

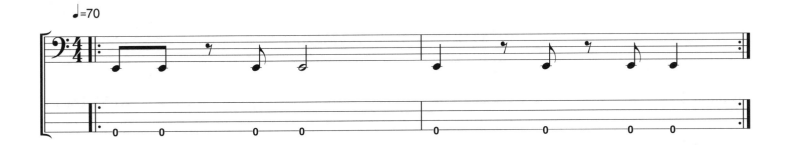

Grade 3 Test 1: Melodic Recall

You will be asked to play back on your instrument a four bar melody composed from the F major pentatonic scale. You will be given the tonic and told the starting note. The test will be played twice with a drum backing. There is a short break for you to practise and then the test will recommence. You will then play the melody in time to the drum backing. The test is continuous.

Example 1   CD 2 Track 1

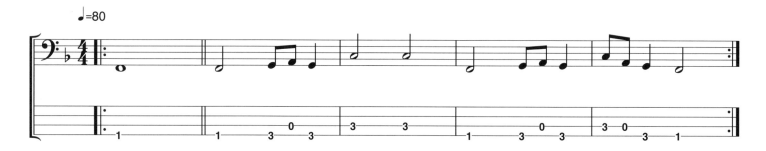

Example 2   CD 2 Track 2

Example 3   CD 2 Track 3

Example 4

Example 5

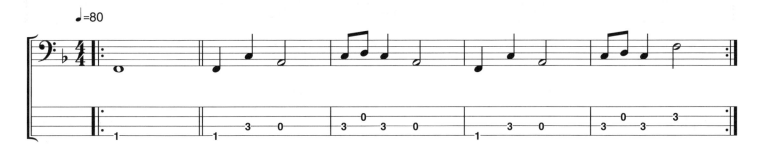

Example 6

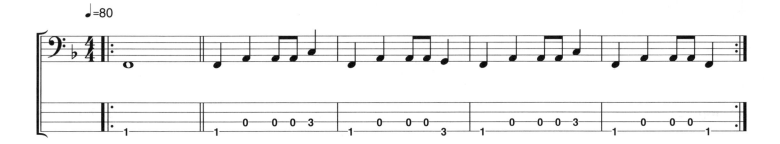

Grade 3 Test 2: Harmonic Recall

You will be asked to play back on your instrument the root notes of a four bar chord sequence played on CD. You will be given the tonic note, told the key, and the sequence is played twice with a guitar and drums backing. There is a short break for you to practise and the test will recommence. You will then play the root notes in time to the guitar and drums backing. The sequence will consist of the chords I, IV, V. The test is continuous.

Example 1   CD 2 Track 7

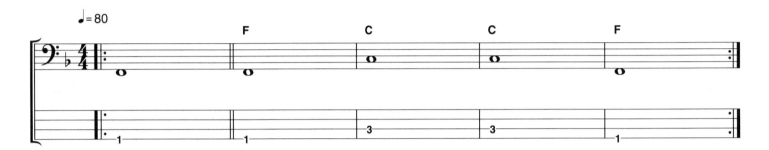

Example 2   CD 2 Track 8

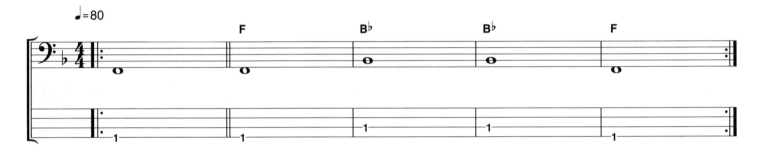

Example 3   CD 2 Track 9

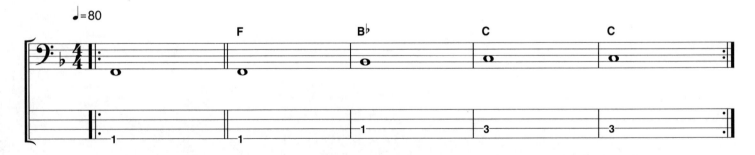

Example 4

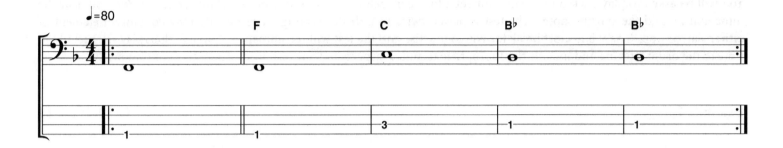

Example 5

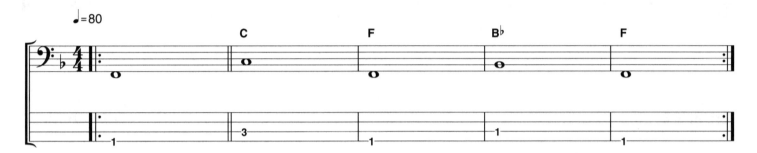

Example 6

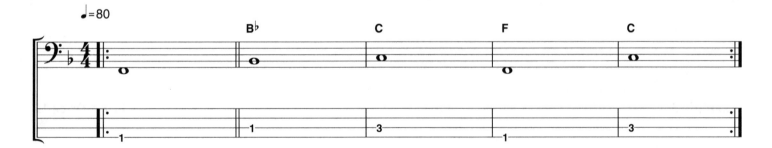

Grade 4 Test 1: Melodic Recall

You will be asked to play back on your instrument a four bar melody composed from the F♯minor scale. You will hear the tonic and be told the starting note. The test is played twice to a drum backing. The melody may contain an element of **either** slap **or** pop. There is a short break for you to practise and the test will recommence. You will then play the melody in time to the drum backing and include the appropriate technical aspects in your response. The test is continuous.

Example 1   CD 2 Track 13

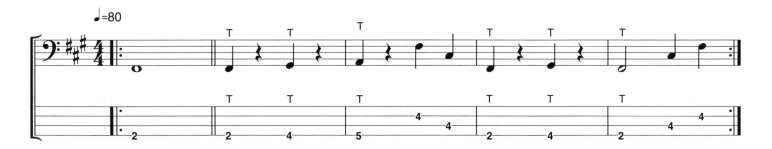

Example 2   CD 2 Track 14

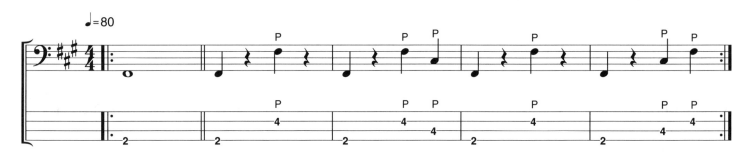

Example 3   CD 2 Track 15

Example 4

Example 5

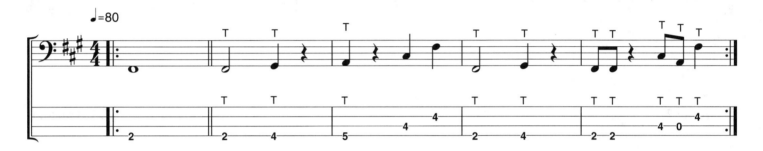

Example 6

Grade 4 Test 2: Harmonic Recall

You will be asked to play back on your instrument the root notes in the given rhythm of a four bar chord sequence played on CD. You will be given the tonic note, told the key, and the sequence is played twice with a guitar and drums backing. There is a short break for you to practise and the test will recommence. The sequence will be in the keys of F#major or minor and consist of the chords I, IV, V. The test is continuous.

Example 1   CD 2 Track 19

Example 2   CD 2 Track 20

Example 3   CD 2 Track 21

Example 4

CD 2 Track 22

Example 5

CD 2 Track 23

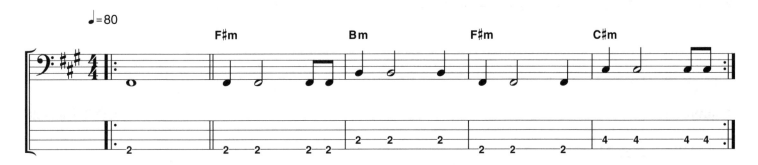

Example 6

CD 2 Track 24

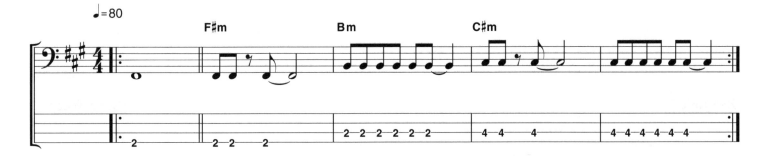

Grade 5 Test 1: Melodic Recall

You will be asked to play back on your instrument a four bar melody composed from the F# major pentatonic scale. You will be given the tonic and told the starting note. The test is played twice to a drum backing. There is a short break for you to practise and the test will recommence. You will then play the melody in time to the drum backing and include the appropriate technical aspects in your response. The test is continuous.

Example 1   CD 2 Track 25

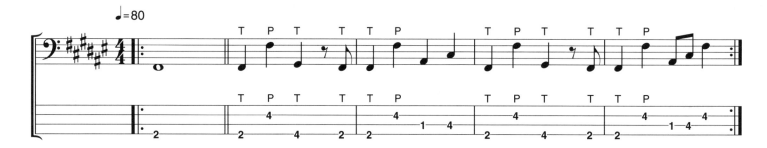

Example 2   CD 2 Track 26

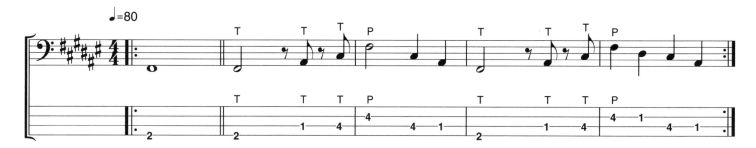

Example 3   CD 2 Track 27

Example 4

Example 5

Example 6

Grade 5 Test 2: Harmonic Recall

You will be asked to play back on your instrument the root notes in the given rhythm of a four bar chord sequence played on CD. You will be given the tonic note, told the key, and the sequence is played twice with a guitar and drums backing. There is a short break for you to practise and the test will recommence. The sequence will be in the keys of F♯ or B♭ major or minor and consist of the chords I, II, IV, V. The test is continuous.

Example 1   **CD 2 Track 31**

Example 2   **CD 2 Track 32**

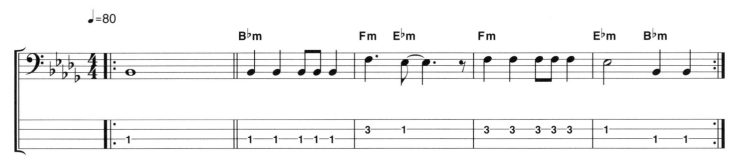

Example 3   **CD 2 Track 33**

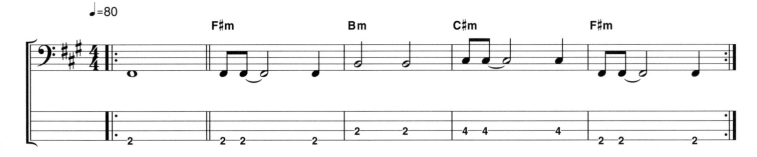

Example 4

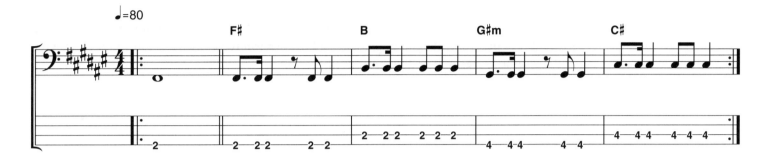

Example 5

Example 6

Grade 6 Test 1: Melodic Recall

You will be asked to play back on your instrument a bassline of four bars scored for guitar, bass and drums and composed in one of the keys of the technical exercises at Grade 6. You will be given the tonic, told the key, and the test is played twice to a full band backing. There is a short break in the test for you to practise and the test will recommence. You will then play the melody in time to the guitar and drums backing. The test is continuous.

Example 1   CD 2 Track 37

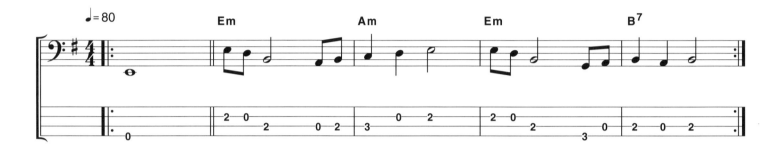

Example 2   CD 2 Track 38

Example 3   CD 2 Track 39

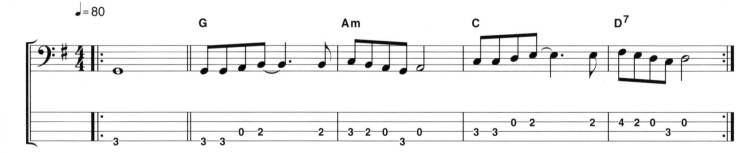

Example 4

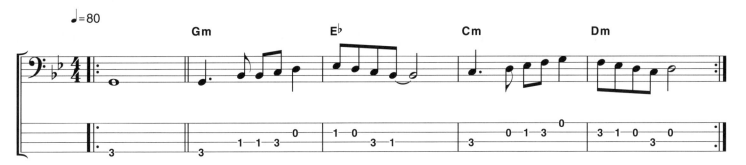

Example 5

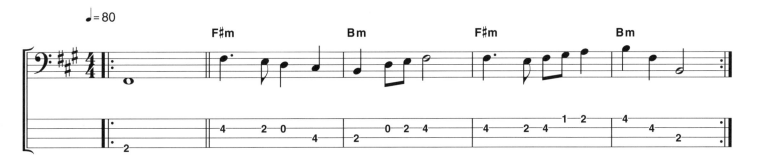

Example 6

Grade 6 Test 2: Harmonic Recognition & Recall

You will be asked to play back on your instrument the root notes and identify the chord types from a four bar chord sequence played on CD. You will be given the tonic note, told the key, and the sequence is played twice. Keys will be taken from the technical exercises at Grade 6.

Example 1   CD 2 Track 43

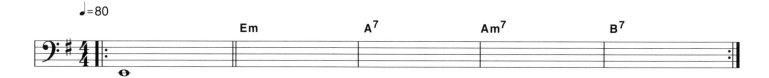

Example 2   CD 2 Track 44

Example 3   CD 2 Track 45

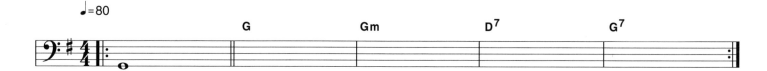

Example 4

Example 5

Example 6

Grade 7 Test 1: Melodic Recall

You will be asked to play back on your instrument a bassline of four bars scored for guitar, bass and drums and composed in one of the keys of the technical exercises at Grade 7. You will be given the tonic, told the key, and the test is played twice to a full band backing. There is a short break in the test for you to practise and the test will recommence. You will then play the melody in time to the guitar and drums backing. The test is continuous.

Example 1   CD 3 Track 1

Example 2   CD 3 Track 2

Example 3   CD 3 Track 3

Example 4

CD 3 Track 4

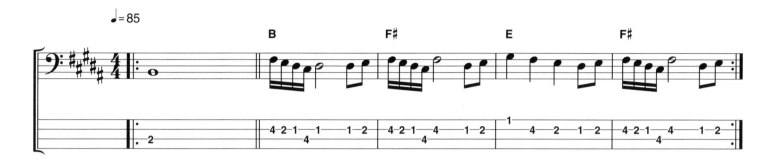

Example 5

CD 3 Track 5

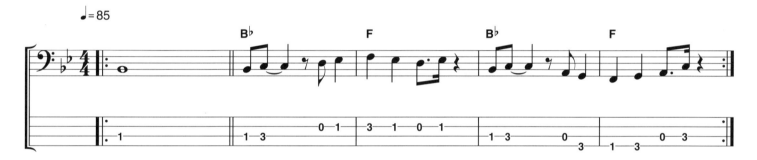

Example 6

CD 3 Track 6

Grade 7 Test 2: Harmonic Recognition & Recall

You will be asked to play back on your instrument the root notes and identify the chord types from a four bar chord sequence played on CD. You will be given the tonic, told the key, and the sequence is played twice. Keys will be taken from the technical exercises at Grade 7.

Example 1   CD 3 Track 7

Example 2   CD 3 Track 8

Example 3   CD 3 Track 9

Example 4

Example 5

Example 6

Grade 8 Test 1: Melodic Recall

You will be asked to play back on your instrument a bassline of four bars scored for guitar, bass and drums and composed in one of the keys of the technical exercises at Grade 8. You will be given the tonic, told the key, and the test is played twice to a full band backing. There is a short break in the test for you to practise and the test will recommence. You will then play the melody in time to the guitar and drums backing. The test is continuous.

Example 1   CD 3 Track 13

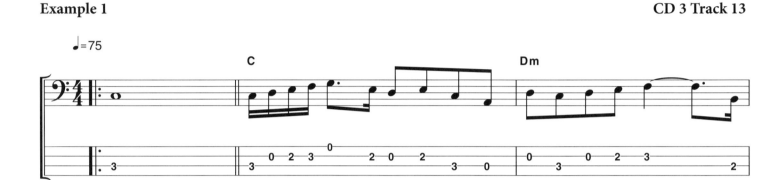

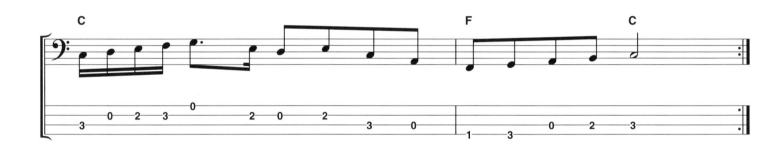

Example 2   CD 3 Track 14

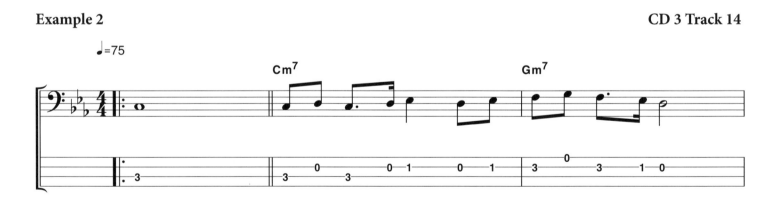

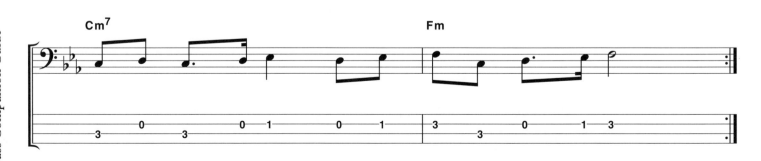

Example 3

Example 4

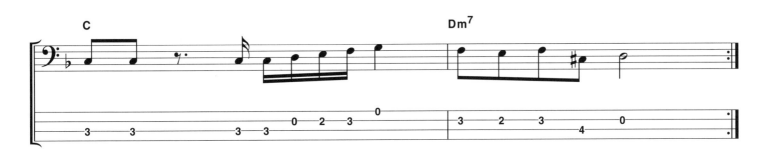

Example 5

CD 3 Track 17

Example 6

CD 3 Track 18

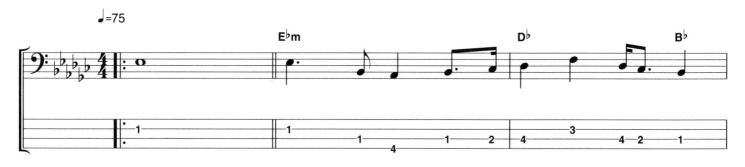

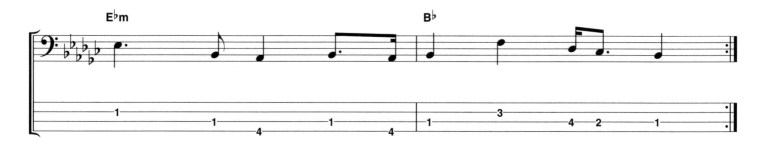

Grade 8 Test 2: Harmonic Recognition & Recall

You will be asked to play back on your instrument the root notes in the given rhythm and identify the chord types from a four bar chord sequence played on CD. You will be given the tonic, told the key, and the sequence is played twice. Keys will be taken from the technical exercises at Grade 8.

Example 1   CD 3 Track 19

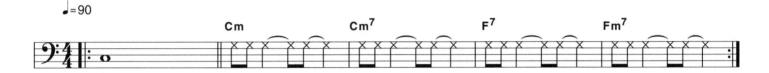

Example 2   CD 3 Track 20

Example 3   CD 3 Track 21

Example 4

Example 5

Example 6

Quick Study Pieces

A quick study piece (QSP) is played in Grade 6, 7 and 8 exams. You will be given a QSP to prepare 20 minutes before entering the examination room. You are asked to arrive at the exam centre at least half an hour before your examination time to give yourself enough time to practise.

You will be asked to perform the QSP from a paper outline and a CD given to you by the examiner. The outline is in the form of a 'lead sheet' or 'session chart' and will contain information on style, tempo and length, along with other musical information such as dynamics and marked solo passages. The QSP is written in standard notation, with TAB fingerings and chord notation.

The CD contains a backing track to be used for both practice and performance in the examination. Each QSP will be in one of the following styles: rock, funk, blues or jazz. The performance should reflect the style of the piece and you should use the 'spaces' in the music to develop your musical ideas.

The full technical specifications for the QSPs can be found in the Bass *Syllabus Guide* on page 22. There are three practice examples of the QSPs by grade shown below and there are two audio tracks on the CD for each one. The first track contains an 'idealised' version of the QSP, while the second track is the backing track for you to play along to.

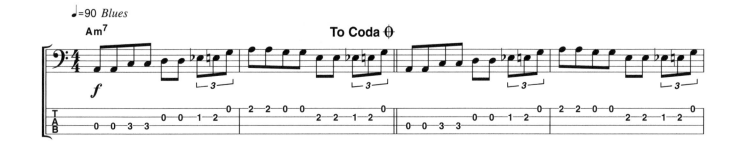

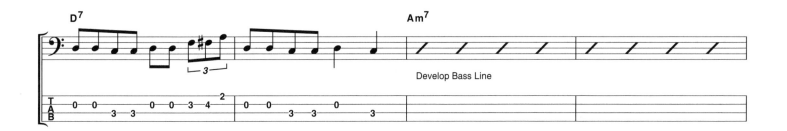

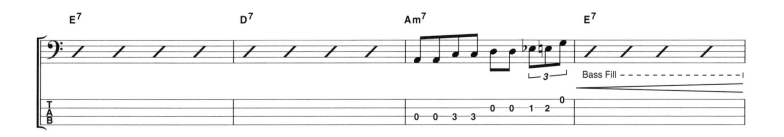

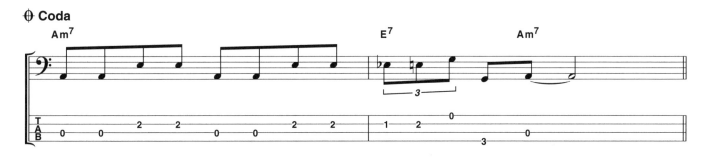

Grade 6 Example 2

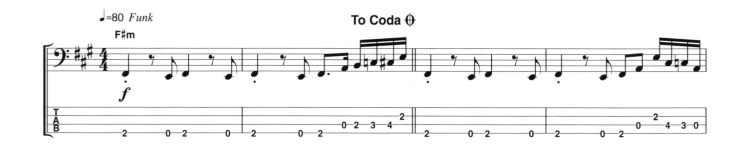

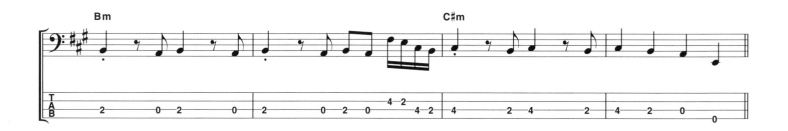

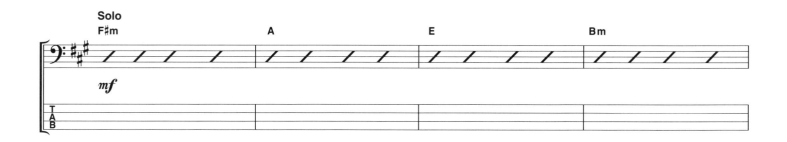

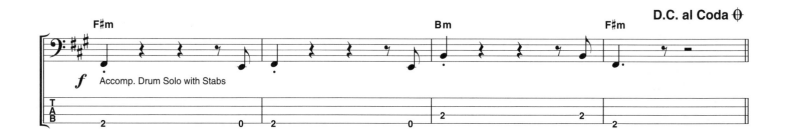

Grade 6 Example 3

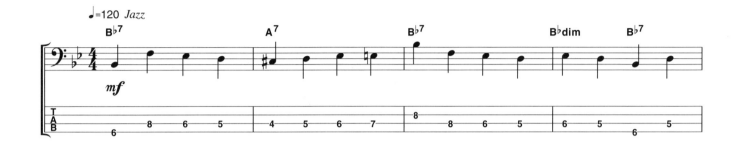

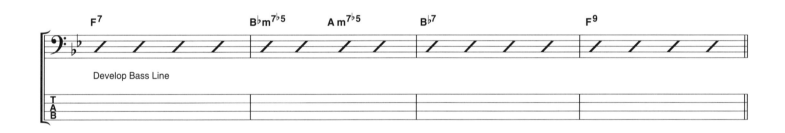

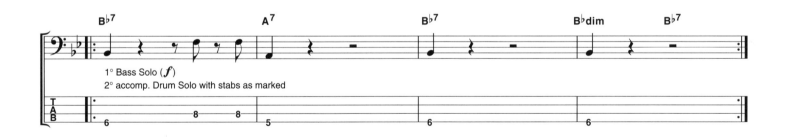

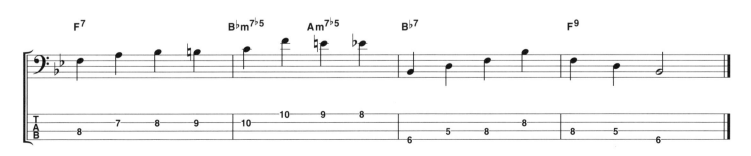

Grade 7 Example 1

Grade 7 Example 2

Grade 7 Example 3

CD 3 Tracks 35 & 36

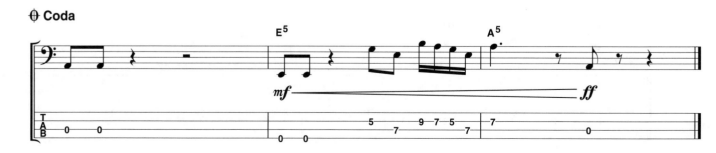

Grade 8 Example 1

Grade 8 Example 2

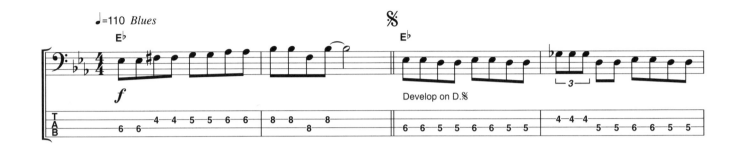

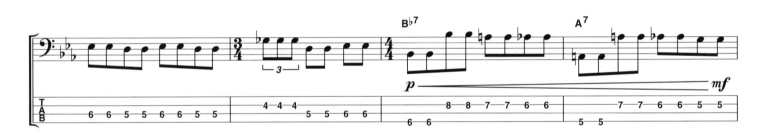

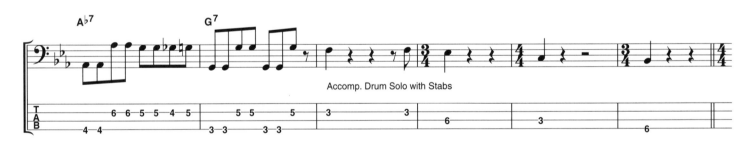

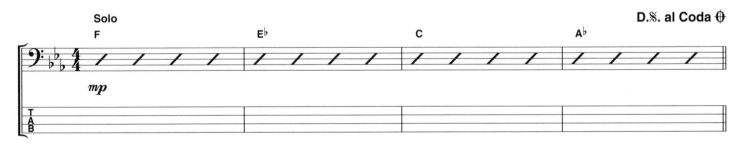

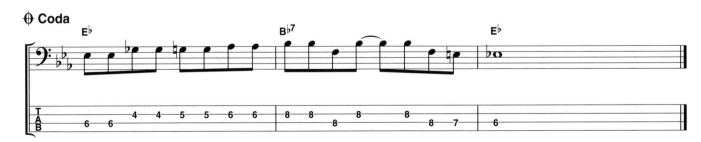

Grade 8 Example 3

General Musicianship Questions

Each Rockschool grade exam ends with five questions asked by the examiner. The examiner will ask you these questions using a piece played by you as a starting point. In Grades 1-6, you will be asked questions in two main areas: (i) music notation and (ii) knowledge of the bass (including amplification). Grades 7 & 8 will include a third category of question concerning history and style.

Here are some sample questions that are typically asked by Rockschool's examiners grade by grade, along with sample answers typically given to examiners by candidates. As a general rule, in Grades 1-3, examiners will ask candidates four questions on the music notation and one instrument question. In Grades 4-6 the instrument knowledge questions may also cover bass amplification and effects. In Grades 7 & 8 you can expect questions to cover all three categories of notation, style and instrument knowledge. Please note that these are indicative questions and that some questions may be asked in more than one grade.

Grade 1

The theory questions here refer to the performance piece 'Fake Tortoise', page 4.

Q: What does 4/4 mean?
A: Four quarter (crotchet) notes in a bar

Q: How many beats is the first note worth?
A: Two beats

Q: What is the pitch of the first note?
A: E

Q: What is the difference between a major and a minor chord?
A: A major chord sounds 'happy' and a minor chord sounds 'sad' OR
A: A major chord has a major third and a minor chord has a minor third

Instrumental question:
Q: Where is/are the nut/pick-ups/neck/frets/controls on your bass?
Q: What are the open notes of the bass?
A: The notes are E, A, D & G

Grade 2

The theory questions here refer to the performance piece 'M & C's Tune', page 6.

Q: what do the two flats at the beginning of the piece mean?
A: It is the key signature

Q: What does 'f' mean?
A: Loud

Q: What value is the rest in the first bar?
A: Quarter (crotchet) note rest

Q: What do these signs mean in bars 5 and 8?
A: Repeat marks

Q: How many beats does the note in bar two of the final line last for?
A: Four beats

Instrument question:

Q: Can you name two bass makes for me?
A: Fender and Gibson

Grade 3

The theory questions here refer to the performance piece 'Pipeline', pages 10-11.

Q: What do the two sets of symbols at the beginning of the first bar refer to?
A: The bass clef and the key signature

Q: What do '*p*' and '*f*' mean?
A: Quiet and loud (*piano* and *forte*)

Q: What does the mark over the second beat in bar 1, line 2 mean?
A: It is a hammer on or slur marking

Q: What does the dot above a note mean?
A: Play the note short or *staccato*

Instrument question:
Q: What do the volume and tone controls do?
A: The volume makes the sound louder or softer and the tone control makes the sound have more treble or more bass, depending on the setting

Grade 4

The theory questions here refer to the performance piece 'Let it Go', pages 12-13.

Q: What does the symbol underneath the note in bar 1 mean?
A: This is an accent marking

Q: What do the markings '*sfz*' mean?
A: Suddenly loud and then quieter, like an accent

Q: What does a line connecting two notes signify?
A: These are tied notes. You play the first note and hold it on for the value of the second note as well

Q: Explain what you do at the D.C. al Coda marking?
A: At this point you return to the beginning and play until you see the Coda sign and then skip to the Coda

Instrument question:
Q: Should you want to get distortion from the amp, how would you go about it?
A: Turn down the volume, turn up the gain

Grade 5

The theory questions here refer to the performance piece 'All Funked Up', pages 10-11.

Q: What do 'T' and 'P' in bar 3 mean?
A: Thumb (Slap) and Pop

Q: What is the key signature of this piece?
A: Three sharps: F♯, C♯, G♯: A major or F♯ minor

Q: How is an F♯ minor 7th chord constructed?
A: F♯, A, C♯ and E

Q: What do you do when you see a notehead is in the form of a cross?
A: The note is muted

Instrument question:
Q: How would you tune your bass without using a tuner?
A: Tune to the fifth fret or use harmonics

Grade 6

The theory questions here refer to the performance piece 'Funkus Regulus', pages 7-9.

Q: This piece has two time signatures, 4/4 and 7/8. What does this mean?
A: Four quarter (crotchet) notes to a bar and seven eighth (quaver) notes to a bar

Q: What are the values of the notes and rests on beats 3 & 4 of bar 1 in line 2?
A: A sixteenth note rest, dotted eighth note tied to a sixteenth note, sixteenth note rest and an eighth note

Q: What are the pitch names of the first two notes?
A: B and D♯

Q: How is a G major 7th chord constructed?
A: The notes are: G, B, D and F♯

Instrument question:
Q:What are the main technical differences between playing a fretted and fretless bass?
A: On a fretted bass, the frets divide the fingerboard into semitone divisions. Fretless basses have a distinct sound because the absense of frets means the strings are pressed down directly onto the fretboard wood. This a particular sound akin to that of a double bass. The fretless bass also allows players to use expressive techniques such as glissando, vibrato and microtonal intonations.

Grade 7

The theory questions here refer to the performance piece 'Chew Boom', pages 10-12.

Q: How are notes with diamond-shaped heads played?
A: As harmonics

Q: What types of harmonics are being used in line 3? And how do you play these?
A: Natural harmonics

Q: The key signature has two sharps. What mixolydian mode has the same two sharps?
A: The mode is A mixolydian

Q: What are the notes of the mode A mixolydian?
A: A, B, C♯, D, E, F♯,G and A

Historical question:
Q: Name a famous bassplayer and tell me something about his style:
A: Jaco Pastorius was an American musician and songwriter widely acknowledged as a virtuoso of the fretless bass. His playing style was renowned for dazzling solos and driving groove lines.

Grade 8

The theory questions here refer to the performance piece 'Some You Win', pages 16-17.

Q: How is a minor 9th chord constructed?
A: Root note, minor 3rd, perfect 5th, minor 7th and 9th

Q: Explain the techniques used in bar 2
A: One note is accented (played louder to highlight it), another is muted (the sound is percussive because the finger is not pressing on the finger board fully) and vibrato, which is a rapid oscillation of the string around one note without actually bending it

Q: How is an F♯ Alt chord made up?
A: F♯, A, C natural and E

Q: What are the notes that make up a diminished scale beginning on B?
A: B, C, D, E♭, F, G♭, A♭, A and B

Q: Tell me about jazz-funk as a style
A: Jazz-funk is a sub genre of jazz music characterised by a strong back-beat and electrified sounds. It is mostly an American genre, where it was popular in the 1970s and early 1980s but British bands were also influenced by it as well. Herbie Hancock, Stanley Clarke, The Jazz Funk Collective and Level 42 are examples of artists and bands that working the genre.

Bass Notation Explained

THE MUSICAL STAVE shows pitches and rhythms and is divided by lines into bars. Pitches are named after the first seven letters of the alphabet.

TABLATURE graphically represents the bass guitar fingerboard. Each horizontal line represents a string, and each number represents a fret.

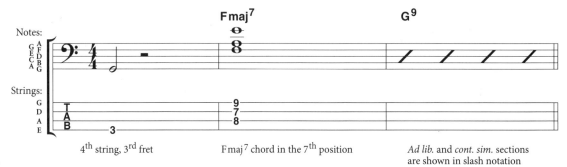

4th string, 3rd fret   Fmaj7 chord in the 7th position   *Ad lib.* and *cont. sim.* sections are shown in slash notation

Definitions For Special Bass Guitar Notation

HAMMER ON: Pick the lower note, then sound the higher note by fretting it without picking.

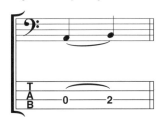

PULL OFF: Pick the higher note then sound the lower note by lifting the finger without picking.

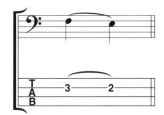

SLIDE: Pick the first note, then slide to the next with the same finger.

GLISSANDO: Pick the note and slide along the string in the direction indicated.

SLAP STYLE: Slap bass technique is indicated through the letters T (thumb) and P (pull).

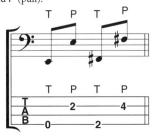

TAPPING: Sound note by tapping the string – circles denote a picking hand tap, squares a fretting hand tap.

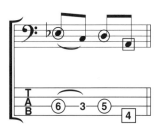

DEAD (GHOST) NOTES: Pick the string while the note is muted with the fretting hand.

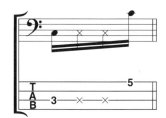

NATURAL HARMONICS: Lightly touch the string above the indicated fret then pick to sound a harmonic.

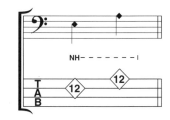

(accent) • Accentuate note (play it louder).

(accent) • Accentuate note with great intensity.

(staccato) • Shorten time value of note.

• Fermata (Pause)

D.%. al Coda

D.C. al Fine

• Go back to the sign (%), then play until the bar marked *To Coda* ⊕ then skip to the section marked ⊕ *Coda*.

• Go back to the beginning of the song and play until the bar marked *Fine* (end).

• Repeat bars between signs.

• When a repeated section has different endings, play the first ending only the first time and the second ending only the second time.